BATS SET I

FLYING FOX BATS

Tamara L. Britton
ABDO Publishing Company

visit us at
www.abdopublishing.com

Printed in the United States of America, North Mankato, Minnesota.
042010
092010

 PRINTED ON RECYCLED PAPER

Cover Photo: iStockphoto
Interior Photos: Alamy p. 15; AP Images p. 5; Getty Images p. 21; iStockphoto pp. 13, 19;
   © Merlin D. Tuttle, Bat Conservation International, www.batcon.org pp. 11, 20;
   Peter Arnold pp. 9, 17

Editor: Megan M. Gunderson
Art Direction & Cover Design: Neil Klinepier

Library of Congress Cataloging-in-Publication Data

Britton, Tamara L., 1963-
  Flying Fox bats / Tamara L. Britton.
      p. cm. -- (Bats)
  Includes bibliographical references and index.
  ISBN 978-1-61613-392-4
  1. Flying foxes--Juvenile literature. I. Title.
  QL737.C575B7524 2011
  599.4'9--dc22
                                    2010009360

CONTENTS

FLYING FOX BATS

There are more than 1,100 species of bats in the world. In the family **Pteropodidae**, 59 species are flying fox bats. Flying fox bats are also called **Old World** fruit bats.

Bats are mammals. One-quarter of all mammals are bats! Like other mammals, bats have hair. And, mother bats give birth to live babies and feed them with milk. Yet, bats can do something no other mammal can do. Bats can fly!

Some people are afraid of bats. But bats are helpful. Insect-eating bats eat millions of pests every year. Bats that eat fruits and flowers help **pollinate** plants. These bats plant trees by scattering fruit seeds as they fly. Each of these helpful creatures is an important part of its ecosystem.

Flying fox bats drink water while flying to and from their roosts.

WHERE THEY'RE FOUND

Bats live all over the world except the polar regions and a few ocean islands. They are found on every continent except Antarctica!

Flying fox bats live in the **tropical** rain forests of Australia and Asia. They also live on islands from Madagascar to Australia, and from Indonesia to Asia.

Bats that live in **temperate** climates **hibernate** during the winter months. Since flying fox bats live in tropical climates, food is always available. So they do not hibernate. But, flying foxes will **migrate** to find ripening fruits.

ASIA

AFRICA

Indian Ocean

Pacific Ocean

Indonesia

Flying Fox
Bat Habitat

Madagascar

AUSTRALIA

N

WHERE THEY LIVE

Flying fox bats live in forests and swamps. They also live on small coastal islands. There, flying foxes make their homes at the tops of tall trees. They **roost** in large groups called camps. Male and female bats roost separately.

A bat roosts by hanging upside down by its feet. Each foot has five toes with sharp, curved claws. To roost, a flying fox grabs a tree branch with its claws. When the bat relaxes, a **tendon** in each foot closes the claws around the branch.

About 100,000 bats can make up a single camp. In camps, the bats do a lot of flapping about and squawking at each other! Sometimes, the camps get so big they damage the trees.

In the past, a camp could contain millions of bats! But habitat and population loss mean today's camps are much smaller.

SIZES

Some bats are very tiny. Kitti's hog-nosed bats grow to only 1 inch (2.5 cm) long. That is about the size of a large bumblebee! Although their bodies are small, their **wingspan** is 6 inches (15 cm).

The smallest flying fox bat is the little golden mantled flying fox. It weighs just 6 ounces (180 g). Its wingspan is 19 inches (50 cm).

The biggest flying fox is also the world's largest bat. The Malayan flying fox can grow more than 16 inches (40 cm) long. It weighs about 2 to 3.5 pounds (1 to 1.5 kg). Its wingspan reaches more than 5 feet (1.5 m)!

Like all bats, the Malayan flying fox is a member of the order Chiroptera. This Greek word means "hand wing." Bats have hands that are also wings!

SHAPES

As their name suggests, flying fox bats look like foxes! Their large heads resemble a fox's head. Flying foxes have small ears and long, pointed snouts. Their large eyes can see very well.

Thick fur covers their heads and bodies. It is mainly grayish brown or black. The fur between their shoulders is often yellow or grayish yellow. Some flying fox species also have stripes on their fur.

A flying fox has two arms. Each arm has a hand with four fingers and a thumb. The thumb has a claw that helps the bat grab and hold fruit. The wings are elastic **membranes**. They stretch between the bat's fingers, body, and legs.

Most bats have short tails. A few, such as rat-tailed bats, have long tails. But, flying fox bats don't have any tail at all!

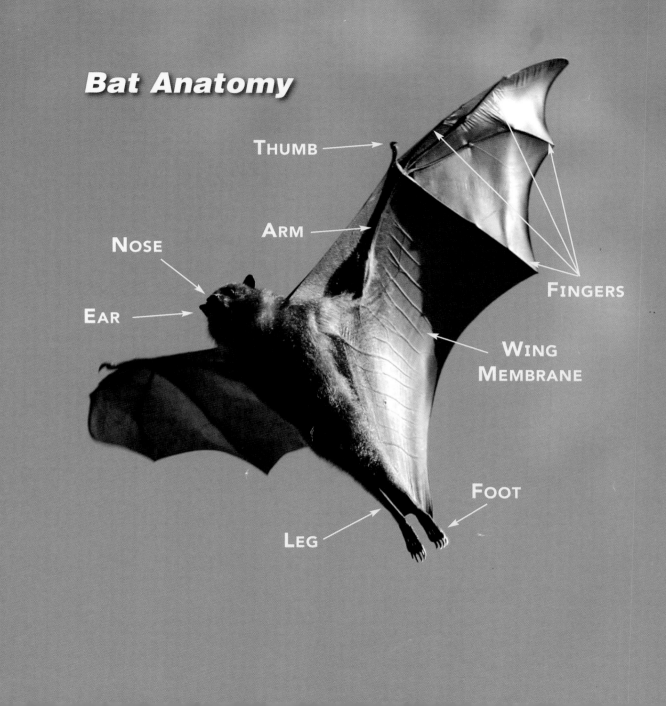

Bat Anatomy

THUMB

ARM

NOSE

EAR

FINGERS

WING
MEMBRANE

FOOT

LEG

SENSES

Flying fox bats can hear, taste, feel, see, and smell. Those are the same five senses you use! Their senses of sight and smell are especially well developed.

Some bats use echolocation to "see" in the dark. To echolocate, they make high-pitched sounds. The sounds go out and bounce off objects such as trees, buildings, or insects.

These sounds return to the bats as echoes. The echoes tell the bats the size and location of objects. Bats use echolocation to fly safely, find food, and avoid danger.

However, flying foxes eat fruit, nectar, and pollen instead of insects. And they live outside in trees, not inside dark caves. So, flying foxes do not echolocate. They don't need to! They use other senses to find food, **roosting** sites, and other bats.

While eating, flying fox bats hold food with their feet or their thumbs.

DEFENSE

Flying fox bats are large, but they still have predators. Cats, dogs, raccoons, and skunks eat bats. Owls, hawks, falcons, snakes, and large frogs also feast on bats. Like most bats, flying foxes are **nocturnal**. So, they avoid predators that hunt by day.

The flying fox's biggest predator is people. Native peoples have always hunted these bats for food. And today, flying fox meat is sold internationally. In some areas, the bats are seen as pests. They damage fruit plantations because they eat so much fruit. So, farmers kill the bats to protect their crops.

Flying fox populations are threatened. Researchers say the Malayan flying fox could be

In some societies, eating flying fox is as common as eating chicken is in other societies.

extinct as early as 2015. In Thailand, laws protect the bats. Governments in other countries where the bats live are considering similar measures.

FOOD

Flying fox bats eat so much fruit they can seem like pests to farmers. Yet, their diet helps keep the ecosystem healthy.

Flying foxes eat fruit, nectar, pollen, and flowers. The bats travel 7 to 8.5 miles (12 to 14 km) each night to locate food. They use their keen eyesight and sharp sense of smell to find it. They prefer brown or green fruits that have a sour or musky scent.

The bats eat the fruit by taking **pulp** into their mouths. They swallow the juice and then spit out the pulp and the seeds. They will swallow some pulp if the fruit is soft, like bananas.

After the bats eat, they pass waste from their bodies as they fly. This scatters even more seeds. The seeds the bats spread grow into new fruit trees. In this way, flying fox bats play an important part in rain forest plant reproduction.

Because of their diet, flying fox bats are also known as fruit bats.

BABIES

In order to continue their role in the ecosystem, bats must reproduce. During mating seasons, both male and female flying fox bats **roost** together. After mating, the males return to their separate roosts.

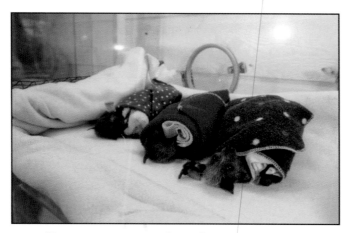

Rescue organizations care for motherless pups until they are old enough to return to the wild.

Most flying foxes have just one baby a year. Some species can have one baby in the spring and another during the rainy season. The baby bats are called pups.

A pup is very big at birth. A newborn bat often weighs 25 percent of its mother's weight! The pup is born with well-developed legs. But, its wings still need time to grow.

After it is born, the pup climbs up onto its mother's chest to nurse. At first, the mother bat takes her baby along when she gathers food. Later, the pup stays behind at the **roost**.

A pup stays with its mother for three to four months. By then, it is able to live on its own. Then, it will seek its own mate and take its place in the forest ecosystem.

GLOSSARY

hibernate - to spend a period of time, such as the winter, in deep sleep.

membrane - a thin, easily bent layer of animal tissue.

migrate - to move from one place to another, often to find food.

nocturnal - active at night.

Old World - all the continents of the eastern half of Earth, except Australia.

pollinate - when birds, insects, or winds transfer pollen from one flower or plant to another.

Pteropodidae (tehr-uh-PAHD-uh-dee) - the scientific name for a family of fruit bats.

pulp - the soft, juicy part of a fruit.

roost - to perch or settle down to rest. A roost is a place, such as a cave or a tree, where animals rest.

temperate - having neither very hot nor very cold weather.

tendon - a band of tough fibers that joins a muscle to another body part, such as a bone.

tropical - having a climate in which there is no frost and plants can grow all year long.

wingspan - the distance from one wing tip to the other when the wings are spread.

WEB SITES

To learn more about flying fox bats, visit ABDO Publishing Company on the World Wide Web at **www.abdopublishing.com**. Web sites about flying fox bats are featured on our Book Links page. These links are routinely monitored and updated to provide the most current information available.

INDEX